The Job Search Book

How to smash that interview
and get the job you really want!

By Chris Bell

Dedication

This book would not have been possible without the love and support from my loving wife and fantastic children who have been there every step of my career and still inspire me every day. This is for you Vanita, Madison and Harrison.

Who should read this book?

Before you get stuck into this book please make sure you join our email list to receive **FREE** regular updates, insights, views and much more by emailing your name to: **support@jobinterviewgamechanger. com** and also follow our Facebook page at **www.facebook.com/ jobinterviewgamechanger**

This book is for every job seeker who is frustrated with the whole job search and interview process and the lack of response or feed back when dealing with recruitment agencies. In this book you will be given a no holds barred overview of exactly how recruitment agencies work and how much they get paid, how to work with them and how to make them work for you. You will also gain some very valuable and powerful tools, insights, tips & tricks and strategies on how to secure the job you really want along with examples and techniques for conducting the best interviews giving you the confidence to turn the tables on the hiring manager and take back some control on the interview process.

We'll provide you with specific examples of the dos and don'ts when applying for and interviewing for jobs. Outline strategies and templates on CV writing, creating your online brand, preparing for and conducting interviews.

Most importantly you will be given the insider's knowledge from an industry expert and gain access to tried and tested strategies to help build your confidence to take control and increase your chances of conducting better interviews and to secure the job you really want!

About the Author

Chris Bell has specialised in professional recruitment for over 25 years and has worked for some of the industry's top recruitment brands in the UK, Australia and Canada and has helped place 1000's of candidates in roles at all levels all over the world. Originally from the UK Chris has travelled extensively across the USA, Canada, Europe, South Africa, South East Asia and has also lived and worked in Australia for 11 years. Over the years Chris has started a number of new recruitment business ventures from start up to becoming successful businesses on behalf of corporate recruitment firms in the UK, Australia and Canada and now runs his own international consultancy **The Design and Construction Recruitment Company** www.dcrc.co.uk

Chris decided to write this book and also establish **The Job Interview Game Changer** after constantly being asked by candidates, friends and family why recruitment agencies never respond or give any feed back to their applications or CVs and also being asked for general job search advice and how to conduct successful interviews and gain offers rather than rejections, so Chris felt that it was time to finally have **someone from "their" side on "your" side.**

Contents

Welcome and Introduction

Firstly I would like to congratulate you for taking this huge step in securing some expert advice on what can be a very daunting and very frustrating process....**getting that job!** I would also like to thank you for investing your time and hard earned money as I know that you will get a huge amount out of this book so please follow the process and stick with it as there's something here for everyone.

There's a massive amount to get through so let's get started:

So the first question you would have asked yourself is "so what does this guy know?"

Well, I have over 25 years experience working within the professional recruitment sector recruiting for clients on some of the world's largest construction projects located in the UK, Dubai, Thailand, Hong Kong, Malaysia, Indonesia, Singapore, Japan, Australia and Canada to name but a few. During this time I've worked for some of the best known specialist recruitment firms working my way from Trainee Consultant up to Operations Director. I've also spent 3 years running an internal recruitment business for one of the world's largest Construction Services companies which has given me an invaluable insight of what it is like to work directly for the client and today I am the proud owner of my own specialist recruitment practice, so I know exactly how the system works. The reason I established the Job Interview Game Changer was because I know what the job seeker also goes through and I know that there are more rejected candidates than successful ones and my aim is to put job seekers back in control and to finally turn the tables on the recruiters and hiring managers. My mission is to **put an expert from their side on YOUR side!**

As a professional recruitment expert I'm constantly being asked by people, even friends and family, why they're not getting positive results or why recruiters don't respond to them or why they never get offered a job after attending numerous interviews. So I decided to write this book and launch the **Job Interview Game Changer** to reverse the role of the recruiter by actually working for the candidate as opposed to working for the company. This book will give you a full no holds barred insight into how recruiters work, how they get paid and why they only focus on certain candidates, which can leave 100's of other applicants out in the cold. I will also give you the tools, strategies and confidence to go out there and nail that job!

Over the years I've placed and worked closely with 1000's of candidates, I've been on more interview panels than I can remember and I've interviewed for almost every level of job from shop floor to board Director so I know exactly what the interviewer and employer are looking for. I've also experienced the process first hand as a candidate myself when changing jobs and have actually utilised recruitment agencies myself to help me find a job and I've often been amazed at how some of these people stay in business.

During this process I've witnessed some excellent interviewing techniques and I've also seen the many mistakes that candidates and employers make during this process, I say employers because this is a **two way street** and I've seen a lot of great companies fail to hire the best candidates because they didn't put in the effort to show case their company and ended up losing good candidates to their competitors who had taken the time and effort to make that candidate want to work for them. Of course this also goes for all the numerous candidates who didn't put in the leg work or make the effort to make themselves stand out from the crowd. Like I say it's a two way street!

So let's run over what you will get from the 8 chapters laid out in this book:

- Firstly you'll be given the insider's knowledge and real facts of exactly how recruitment agencies work, how they get paid and just how much they get paid – believe me you will be surprised! Also how they select and work with candidates and the reasons why they reject or ignore so many others.

- We will look at how to make recruiters notice you and actually work for you.

- We'll look closely and honestly at you, your approach and the type of job or career you are really looking to secure.

- We'll then take a close and honest look at your brand, meaning your CV, social network profile, how you come across to friends, colleagues as well as current or potential employers.

- At the end of each chapter I will also give you some examples of the types of rookie mistakes I've seen over the years and also some interesting facts that can help you understand the process a lot better.

- Finally I will give you the tools and confidence to create a call to action that will help you focus on finding the job you really want and to stop scatter gunning CVs and actually hone in on the real opportunities and how to get them.

So once again congratulations! You've taken a huge step forward and remember you're not alone there's 1000's of frustrated job seekers out there experiencing the same issues but YOU'VE taken action and you will get real value from this book, so please enjoy the content, take your time and take it all in and do with it as you will but please remember.....**you can only make things happen by taking action yourself.**

Chapter 1: Agencies & Recruiters – *The Insider's Guide*

Welcome to chapter 1 – **Agencies & Recruiters** – this is a great way to start this book as you're about to gain a real insight into exactly:

1. **How recruitment agencies work, how they get paid and just how much and where they focus their efforts?**

2. **Which agencies to work with, how to work with them and how to get them to work for you?**

3. **Key questions to ask your recruiter.**

So let's take a closer look at recruitment agencies:

The recruitment sector is a multibillion dollar industry and is a worldwide business with agencies represented in every country and across every industry sector. Companies or clients pay millions each year to recruitment firms to secure the very best talent on the market and it's very competitive. By investing so much money they want the agency to take away the hassle of advertising, searching, selecting, interviewing, offering and negotiating with candidates so that they can focus on whatever it is their business is there to do, so agencies charge a premium to do this because it can also be extremely costly not to have the right people in the right roles. Recruiters also help the company with how it sells itself and can add value to the interview process and often conduct the interview alongside or on behalf of the company to give them the confidence and the use of a professional interviewer.

Interesting fact; Did you know that there are also recruitment agencies who specialise in recruiting for recruitment firms! They're paid by recruitment experts to go out and find the best recruiters for their recruitment business. Ironic I know but this is also a massive business.

So how do agencies work?

The majority of agencies get paid on what we call "success only" meaning that they'll only get paid once the successful candidate starts work for the client so this can mean a lot of leg work by the recruiter which could result in no fee if they fail to place someone in the role. Whilst this will make the recruiter work harder to fill the role it can also mean that some recruiters will only focus on candidates that they can actually place and will make them money and this can leave some candidates feeling left out in the cold. But you must also understand that recruiters get 100's of responses for each job they advertise and a large number of CVs don't even come close to matching the requirement and they just don't have the time or resources to deal with every single enquiry. The recruiter is trained to scan through CVs very quickly and the average time recruiters take to read a CV is around 6 to 8 seconds and if they don't see something that catches their eye then it will go in the "not suitable" folder.

Agencies come in all shapes and sizes and some specialise in one particular market which we call the "specialist" and also those who cover everything the "generalist" the bigger agencies tend to have specialist divisions such as Accountancy, Finance, Construction, Industrial etc etc. They build databases of 1000's of candidates with the view of being able to offer their clients the "companies" a fast solution to filling their vacancies. To find candidates, recruiters advertise online, in the press, TV, radio and various other media, they also work on referrals offering other candidates IPads, tablets, watches, vouchers and even cash for referrals that they place. Most recruiters will also head hunt, this means targeting someone already in the role they're looking to fill who is currently working for a competitor of their client, they'll approach them and entice them into discussing a possible move. Recruiters are very active on social network sites such as LinkedIn, Twitter etc and build huge networks of potential candidates, clients and contacts they can approach for referrals.

The agency then introduces the candidate to the client, they meet, if all goes well the candidate will be offered and the candidate starts work... simple! This is when the agency gets paid and on the day the candidate starts work for the client the agency will send an invoice to the client. Happy Days!

So how do agencies and their recruiters get paid?

Well some of you might be surprised to hear this and you'll see why it's such big business. Firstly the agency will charge a percentage of the candidate's annual salary as their fee; for example if the company offered the candidate $30,000 then the agency would charge around 15 to 20% (depending on the agreement with their client) of this amount to the client. So in this case $4,500 or if at 20% then the fee would be $6,000. Fees and salary levels differ for each market sector but to give you some examples some recruiter's fees would average $15,000 per placement and they would place 2 to 3 candidates per month and bearing in mind that some of the bigger recruitment firms hire 100's of consultants with each averaging $15,000 per month minimum.......well you do the math! At the other end of the spectrum, I recently met a recruiter who specialises in placing Hedge Fund Managers in London and his average fee to his client per placement is.................$200,000!!! He only places a few of these a year but I think you get the idea...**this is big business!**

Each consultant is targeted by their employer (the agency) to bill a certain amount each month so they generally look to be placing 2 to 3 candidates per month to meet or exceed their financial target of which they then get paid a commission or bonus against, which again would be a percentage of what they've billed that month and in some cases can be up to 40% of billings. So you can see why they're keen to focus their time and efforts on candidates they can actually place.

The key for candidates is to have a recruitment expert on their side, someone who can coach you and give a professional honest opinion and advice on what's working and what's not working. But of course no candidate in their right mind will pay 15% of their salary to an agency and in fact it's illegal for agencies to charge candidates a fee for placing them, however they can charge for other services such as career consultations, CV writing, interview training, coaching etc and some are charging 1000's of dollars for career counselling especially at the executive end of the market.

The best way to approach working with recruiters is to find two firms who specialise in your market sector. Pick up the phone and have a conversation with the relevant consultant and give them a brief bullet point overview of your background but don't give away too much, make this a "teaser" for them to want to know more and say that you're about to come on to the market and looking for a new role and want to select the best agency to represent you. Then ask them about their experience and what they can do for you, we'll cover this in more detail a little later. They will always want to see your CV first but try and tie them down to a meeting and suggest that because you're new to this and do not want your employer or past employer knowing you're looking you'd prefer to have a face to face discussion. You could even say that because you've only just started looking you have yet to write a CV and in fact was hoping they could help with this to ensure you get it right. Unless they're very particular most recruiters would take these as positive signs and take the chance to meet you....they will probably ask you to get a CV together in the meantime but take it with you rather than send it.

The key to working with your chosen recruiter is communication. Make sure that you are very clear and in agreement on the level of role, type of company, location, salary level etc that you want to secure. Also agree which companies this recruiter will be sending your details to and get them to email this to you and to also agree in writing that they will not send your details to any other company without your prior approval, unless you're happy with them spamming your CV across the market. If you do decide to utilise two recruiters at the same time then be very open with them both and let them know they have a little competition but also inform the other which companies you and the other agency are approaching, this way your details will not be sent to the same company by two different recruiters. Believe me this is very common and creates issues all the time for recruiters and it doesn't do anything positive for you as the job seeker. It's a major bug bare for recruiters when they ask the candidate "so have you or anyone on your behalf ever applied to ABC Ltd in the past?" The candidate answers "No, never" so the agent sends in the CV and the client responds saying "we received that candidate's details from another recruiter last week plus they also applied directly on our website!!"

Find a good recruiter and agree the best strategy for you and ask them which companies they already have good relationships with, what current vacancies match your background, realistic salary levels and terms, agree timescales and the action to be taken and by when. Get them to agree to call you by a certain date with an update. Again we'll cover this in more detail shortly.

Some specialist recruiters have often worked in the same role or market sector that they now recruit for which gives them great insight and experience and can add great value to both their clients and candidates. These recruiters can also give you great advice on the types of roles you might not have particular experience in but are looking to explore and they'll give you pointers on how to move into that role/market.

Also good recruiters who have excellent relationships with their clients (meaning they visit them on a regular basis, they know the key decision makers well, they know the 5 year plan of the business, they know what type of people they look out for etc) can often pick up the phone and speak to their contact and arrange an interview without even sending a CV! So find a good, experienced and well connected consultant as they'll work hard to place a good candidate. The best recruiters will always think long term, "candidates become clients and clients become candidates!" and of course good people always refer good people.

Recruiters always need new candidates but they are bombarded by spammed CVs of people who don't meet their needs all the time, so they can often seem ruthless. The key is to find one that specialises in your market sector as they will want to work for you and it's a much better approach rather than just firing out a CV and hoping they will call you.

Once you have a potential recruiter on the hook, some of the key questions you could ask them to establish if they're the one for you:

- What are your specialist sectors?
- Who are your top 5 clients in this sector?
- Which ones do you work for exclusively?
- What is your conversion rate from interview to placement?
- How many placements have you made with these clients in the past 6-12 months?
- What vacancies do you currently have that match my requirements?
- How often will you communicate with me and how?

- What advice or assistance can you give me regarding my CV and application?
- What advice or assistance can you give me regarding interviews?
- What time scales do you believe we are working with to find me a position?
- What will be your strategy for finding me the right position?
- If a recruiter calls you always ask them where they got your name from.

As I stated at the beginning, I've worked for recruitment agencies for the best part of my career and I love what I do especially now that I work for myself. The majority of recruiters and the firms they work for are excellent at what they do and they really do add massive value to both candidates and the companies they represent and whilst it can be argued that they get paid a huge amount of money for what they do, the majority of the time it's worth it as companies can spend hundreds of thousands or millions each year advertising, searching, pre-screening, interviewing, rejecting, hiring etc to find the best people for their businesses and recruitment firms help cut out the hard work and time by doing this on their behalf and the majority of the time will not get paid until the successful candidates commences work so there's risk involved as well.

I've always enjoyed working in recruitment and that's why I still do it but unfortunately as with any other industry you care to think of, there are always going to be a bad few who take advantage and shine a negative light on what is actually a very valuable and much needed business. As well as being a very profitable industry, which also adds incredible value to the world economy not to mention adding value to many people's lives and careers as well as helping grow and develop businesses. At the end of the day it's completely your choice whether to utilise a recruiter or not but if you work with the right one they can also open up a lot of doors and opportunities you didn't know existed.

Rookie Mistake #1:   **"Sending my CV to 10 agencies will increase m y chances of success"....wrong!** If anything it can cause confusion and often result in your CV being sent to the same company multiple times which doesn't make you look good. It's better to work with 1 to 2 agencies and be open with them about who else you're dealing with - this can make them more pro-active if they know they have some competition. Also a trained eye can spot a spammed CV a mile off and unless your CV really sticks out and happens to match the role they're working on the chances are you'll not hear back or you'll receive the standard response that your CV will be kept on file for future consideration.

Interesting Fact: **It's estimated that 70% of vacancies are not advertised** – agencies can often create an opportunity or a vacancy if they have a strong enough relationship with their client and present CVs that aren't linked or related to any vacancy. Good recruiters will know their client's business plans and the types of people they will be looking for should they come along, therefore are often able to secure an interview and create interest out of nothing.

Chapter 2: Get Your Head in the Game!

Welcome to chapter 2 – Get your Head in the Game – whilst recruiters generally are not qualified Psychologists (although I have met a few and they do make very good interviewers and recruiters!) they're great at studying people and are fast to pick up specific habits or traits that people show in their actions, so in this chapter we'll take a close look at:

1. Psychology, strategy and focus

2. Change the way you think – it's a two way street!

3. SWOT yourself!!

Before we jump into this chapter let's just recap on what we covered in chapter 1.

The overall objective of chapter 1 was to give you the background and knowledge of exactly how recruitment agencies work, how they get paid and how they focus their attentions on certain candidates. We also looked at how to select and work with a recruiter that specialises in your sector and to not scatter gun your CV as it will stick out like a sore thumb. This information and way of working should give you more confidence when dealing with and working with recruiters.

OK let's crack on with chapter 2. **Get your Head in the Game**

If there's one thing that really let's a candidate down at interview it's coming across as unprepared, disorganised or just as bad seeming arrogant and therefore not really interested in the job, the company or the opportunity. Sure they might say that they really want the job but there are two types of candidates that show up to interview;

Candidate #1; They say they have good intentions and really want this job, however the alarm clock didn't go off, the car wouldn't start, I was going to do my research last night but the wi-fi went down bla bla bla, I've heard them all before and I have friends who still use these excuses and try and reverse the blame onto something or someone else other themselves. I've known people who just didn't bother turning up because they had a big night........TIME WASTERS!

And then there's Candidate #2; Who's fully researched the company days before, knew the backgrounds of the interviewers, had travelled to the building the day before so they knew the exact time it took to get there, which route to take and where to park, they arrived stress free and ready for the interview. When asked what they knew about the company, they had a short verbal presentation prepared and a list of relevant questions where as candidate #1 left their questions on the train!

You might think I'm exaggerating but believe me this does happen and whilst I know we're all human and shit happens, you do need to do something about it and try and rescue the situation If something really does happen and you think you could be even one minute late for your interview you MUST call ahead and warn them that you will be late, this will go a long way. Seriously whatever your excuse, being late for an interview can be a really bad start to the meeting and not really caring about it can show arrogance and a lack of respect, so at least taking the time and effort to let them know will show some common courtesy and will really help. Like I say shit does happen.

Another real but yet very common let down by the unprepared candidate is when the interviewer asks "What do you know about our company?" and the candidate replies "not a lot really" or "only what the agency told me" or "just what's on your website".........**PLEASE DO NOT DO THIS!** This shows that you have absolutely no interest or couldn't be bothered to look and that you're just going through the motions. With all the information in the world at your finger tips especially company information you have no excuse not to conduct your research. Furthermore surely you would want to know about the company you're about to spend more time with than you do with your family not to mention relying on them to be able to pay you! You don't have to give war and peace or a power point presentation but some key headlines such as; when the company was established and by whom, the company's key products or specialist services, locations, turnover and profit etc will be enough to show you've taken an interest. You will be amazed at how much information you can find especially now with sites such as LinkedIn, Facebook etc and the best place to start of course is the company's show case.....their website. With all the resources available you can find background information on key people in the company, photos, previous employers etc all of which will give you something to present or even use an opener to the interview to help break the ice for example; "Hello Mr Interviewer I read that you used to work with Mr Candidate Senior at ABC Ltd for 8 years, I'm Mr Candidate Junior and he sends his regards" Even noticing the cars in the car park, pictures on the walls, trophies, golf clubs in the corner etc. can all be great ways of starting up the conversation about something a little lighter than the actual interview and will not only put you at ease but they will feel it as well.

Arrive in "peak state" Anyone who has read Tony (Anthony) Robbins will know exactly what this means. Basically, arriving in "peak state" means that you show up as the person who already does this job and should be working for this company. Even if you've not actually done the role before, get yourself in the zone and thinking that you're already in that role and working for their top competitor and they will do what it ever takes to secure you for their company. You've researched the role, the company, the people and their future plans and opportunities and coupled with your personality, smart appearance, early arrival, well thought out questions you will impress and show them that you're the one that they want.

I better get my disclaimer in quick! Now don't get me wrong, don't go overboard here, I'm not saying I want you to come across as arrogant and that you're the dog's doo dahs! All we're looking for here are ways to boost your confidence, knowledge or ability to show understanding and be able to ask relevant questions and present an image of the type of person that they want for their company. I'm not saying lie on your CV or go in and actually pretend that you work for their competitor – it's all in the mind and is confidence building.

One of the best ways I find when coaching candidates on interview techniques and how to boost their confidence is to explain in very simple terms that the interview process is a **two way street**.......yep you heard me, a two way street. What I mean is this; whilst candidates are battling each other to secure the limited number of vacancies there are out there, companies are also battling amongst themselves to secure the best candidates the market has to offer. Therefore they also have to work hard to impress YOU. This is one of the reasons they might use recruiters because they can often sell the company better than the company itself. As well as working with 1000's of candidates on how to sharpen up their brand, interview techniques etc I've also worked with numerous companies who have been wondering why they have had so many offers turned down and the candidates have joined the competition, sometimes for less money. It doesn't take long to discover the key reasons behind this. When asked this question by a client I would always suggest that I sit in on an interview or accompany a candidate to a random interview as an observer and go through the whole process. Below are just a small number of examples of what the candidates had experienced which I report back to the CEO or MD, which always surprised them:

- Receptionist who comes across rude or abrupt and more interested in their phone conversation or other distractions and treated the candidate like he was imposing and maybe in the wrong place, basically the first impression was very poor.

- The interviewer coming to get us 15 minutes later than the scheduled interview and coming across as not too bothered, didn't apologise, seemed rushed and then discovered he hadn't booked a room so we had to sit in reception and conduct the interview there with people walking past and perched on the edge of seats.

- Unprepared interviewer who couldn't even remember the name of the person they were interviewing and had to print off their CV and had obviously done no preparation.

- Interviewer unable to give a confident or factual sell of the company or their business to the candidate or be able to give any real good reasons why the candidate should chose them over their competition when asked.

- Being told at the start of the interview that the other candidate they'd just interviewed was ideal for the role so this had better be impressive.

The list is too long for this book and whilst actually some of the points are very funny this is also incredibly frustrating and very serious because companies and some of their representatives are very complacent and good candidates will turn down offers for reasons other than money and usually it's because how they were treated or what they experienced at the interview. In fact I and other recruiters will often refuse to work with these types of companies who do not identify or address these types of issues. Instead of sending them our candidates we'd do the complete opposite and take candidates out of these companies, they're full of people who probably get treated the same way but as employees. **I could see this developing into a separate book that I could sell to companies!**

In conclusion to this point; remember when you attend an interview the company is also on show and selling themselves to you. Ask yourself and take note such as; how easy was it to get to from your home, how easy was it to park, what is the building and surrounding facilities like, notice how people act in the company such as the receptionist or other people you come across in reception, corridors or when walking through the office, factory, yard etc listen out for comments or conversations to get a feel for the morale – you'll be surprised what you pick up. Also look at the decor, the carpets, the desks, computers, interview rooms, facilities, workshops, yard etc would you like to spend the majority of your day there and I would even take a trip to the toilet and check out these facilities. If not offered a tour during the interview go ahead and ask for one at the end so that you can see where you'd sit/work, the kitchen facilities, storage, the views from the windows, plants, air conditioning etc. You have every right to ask for a tour and what have they got to hide? Whilst a lot of companies don't really care about their appearance others really make the effort to make people want to be there and enjoy being there. Just look at some of the companies like Google, Apple etc a lot of companies have followed suit and are very proud to promote the working/play/rest environment, why not! One of the best offices I worked in had a snooker table, darts board, Xbox, wide screen TV, DVD player and we'd finish at 3pm with an open bar every Friday afternoon.

Like I say it's a two way street – interviewers expect YOU to show up on time, smart, prepared and ready to show off your skills and likewise you should expect the same from them.

Another great way to give yourself confidence and a head start ahead of any curve ball questions from interviewers on your suitability or areas of your CV is to conduct a SWOT analysis on yourself. In this instance a

SWOT is when you look at the role you're interviewing for and compare yourself and experience by looking at your Strengths, Weaknesses, Opportunities and Threats examples could be;

STRENGTHS: 5 years in a similar role working for a major competitor, live 20 minutes from the office and know the area well, I also know 3 people currently in the team and would add great value and strength going forward etc etc etc.

WEAKNESSES: CV shows you spent the last 2 years out of this sector – (always overcome a negative with a positive) this is because I was offered a great opportunity to advance my skills in another role and sector which was a great learning curve for me and I certainly rose to the challenge, however I always intended on returning to what I do and like best and I feel that the time away and the new skills I've learnt will only add value to my skill set.

OPPORTUNITIES: For me securing this job - Long term career development, great training, exciting prospects, great working environment etc etc etc. For you the employer hiring me – A future leader of the business, great motivator, trainer and leader of others, previous clients/ business I can bring to the table etc etc etc.

THREATS: Other candidates with more recent experience – I have the experience from previous roles and the time spent away will only add value and motivate me to exceed my previous successes etc etc etc.

Conducting this exercise prior to the interview can also help you answer some of the questions from interviewers such as what are your weaknesses or why they should pick you over our other candidates etc.

On the flip side; you can also ask the interviewer to do a SWOT on the company. What are their strengths compared to their competition, what are their areas of weakness and how are they addressing these, what opportunities are there for someone like you if you were to join them and what threats are there to the business such us; oil prices, competition, economy, lack of good people, losing key clients etc etc etc.

This exercise can be very revealing! It can also show the interviewer that you're taking a real interest and it can also help guide you with your questioning and help decide if this is the right role or company for **YOU**. Remember two way street!

So get your head in the game - The key thing to remember is that we're all human and we all have the same emotions, some of us just show them more than others. It's easy to say this but you really should try and enjoy the experience. Interviews are normally just a conversation with challenging questions thrown in. So as long as you tell the truth and make sure you research, prepare and have a strategy for how you want the interview to go then you should also gain some control and confidence in how the meeting will work out. Remember that the person you're meeting has a job to do and will make you work for it, so make them work too.

We'll discuss later in another chapter but if you do not get offered the job make sure you take the time to ask the interviewer why you were not successful so you can learn from it. Most good interviewers would be happy to give constructive feed-back but most people throw their toys out of the pram and don't bother asking.

If you utilise everything that you learn in this book I have no doubt that you will think and act very differently towards interviews – don't fear them, use them to learn and train yourself ready to nail the next one!

Rookie Mistake #2:	**"The interviewer is in full control and the candidate has to toe the line and be led by them"** – If you know your strengths and weaknesses and truly believe that you are a strong candidate then you must realise that this is a two way street. The company is also on show and you need to ask them questions to satisfy your needs as well, so go ahead ask them.
Interesting Fact:	Captain Obvious but interviewers are also humans and they've also been through this process at some point in their career. They also know that good people are very hard to come by and therefore they have to work hard and impress you to join their company over their competition, so make them work for it! This will give you much more confidence and some control over the interview process.

Chapter 3:   Your Brand – *Stand out from the crowd*

Welcome to chapter 3 – Your Brand – In this 3rd chapter we'll explore
and take a very close look at your brand, YOU! Basically when it comes
down to it when you're applying for a new job, you're competing with
many other candidates who are also trying to entice potential employers to
select, interview and employ them so you have to think of yourself as your
product that the employer is going to want to buy. Therefore we're going to
look at:

1. How you present yourself – in person and online including Face book,
    LinkedIn, Twitter etc

2. Examples of bad Vs Good

3. Take Action – Take an honest look at how others see you before they
    even meet you, which could be why you're not getting interviews

Before we dive in let's just recap what was covered in chapter 2. Get your
head in the game was all about realising that we're all human and that the
interview is a two way street. Thinking ahead of the game, researching
and preparing well in advance for interviews will give you much more
confidence and power at interviews. Thinking this way will also have an
effect and help you with this next chapter when we look at developing your
brand.

Onto chapter 3; Your Brand....

So what do I mean by your brand, well your "personal brand" will affect
other people's perception, expectation and reaction to you even before you
meet and of course when you actually meet for the first time face to face.

It's a very interesting subject as a lot of people don't really give too much
thought to this and think that their CV and how they dress on the day is
what potential employers are looking at especially prior to actually meeting
them they feel that CV presentation will be all they need to consider, this
is pure complacency and is a big reason why some candidates never get to
the interview stage. Even before the internet a good interviewer/recruiter
would conduct some form of research prior to the interview and of course
all you have to do nowadays is just enter a name into Google and I think
you know the rest.

The majority of people have some form of online profile which of course
can be a good or a bad thing, a double edged sword. Again people's
opinion or attitude to this really differs but the fact is that whether you
agree with it or not, what you think of as your "private" Facebook page,
photos and posts are in reality in the public domain as soon as you push
"post" and therefore anyone can access that information at anytime and
potential employers and interviewers will check you out. Now I'm not

saying that all your Facebook photos should show you in a suit playing chess or having cups of tea with your mother but be honest and put yourself in the place of an employer and you see photos of your potential new employee and representative of your company drunk, exposing themselves, posting inappropriate images and material or telling all their friends how much they hate their job and that their boss is a complete..... well, again I think you get the picture and you may think I'm exaggerating but this is very common. I'm not just talking about Facebook as I've seen a number of people who have what I feel are pretty risky or unsuitable profile photos on LinkedIn which is more for business purposes and where they're trying to attract or entice potential customers or employers!

Having employers looking at your online information and posts was challenged in the courts not so long ago but it's very hard to stop this seeing as you have made the information "public" domain so it's very hard to stop anyone looking at it. One point I would make is that I have heard stories of candidates and actual employees being asked by interviewers or managers to submit their Facebook passwords which I would strongly suggest you do not do. At the end of the day it's purely your choice how you live your life and what you decide to post on the internet and I'm certainly not here to preach to you. However if you're very serious about the type or level of role you're aiming to secure then also think very seriously about "your brand" which is what you're selling and how you will come across to potential employers. We'll cover some of these in more detail in other chapters but some key things to think about:

- Spelling and grammar on covering letters, CVs etc – this does matter and mistakes are noticed so please take the time to get it right.

- Content on CVs – we'll cover this later but CV's should generally be 3 pages maximum and to the point, you shouldn't overload with needless information or photos or attach endless certificates – if they're needed they'll be asked for later.

- Facebook, Twitter etc accounts – look at your photos and posts and be honest about how you really come across, it's very easy to clean these up. Start with making sure your profile picture is recent and not from 10 years ago.

- LinkedIn profile – this is an important one which I'll come back onto later.

- Email and Twitter addresses – if you're sending your CV to a potential employer from your davebigboy@ or drugsandalcohol@ or sexylady@ or Ilovetoparty@ you might put some people off. It's easy and free to have as many email accounts as you want so why not set up a separate email account for your job search and give it a professional address

- Dress code at interview – This is covered in more detail later but some say dress for the job you're going for but I believe it's always better to overdress for an interview rather than guess and feel very uncomfortable because everyone else is in a suit and you're in your jeans and rock band T-Shirt. If you're not 100% sure you could always call and ask what the dress code is, nothing wrong with this at all. Always make sure you're wearing the correct shoes and that they're clean as some people have a real thing about how people keep their shoes!

- Personal appearance – hair, facial hair, ironed clothes etc are all things that need attention. If you've overslept and dashed to the interview with facial stubble, un-ironed shirt and scuffed shoes you won't be looking or even feeling your best. My old boss used to say "look smart, feel smart!" good advice really

- Body language, hand shake and eye contact – we'll cover this in the interview chapter

- Vocabulary, talking and listening balance – We have 2 ears and 1 mouth and they should be used in that order. Never speak at interview to fill what might appear uncomfortable silences. I've always liked the saying "better to remain silent and have people only think that you're stupid rather than open your mouth and confirm that you are!"

Time for you to do some work now, you will be asked to refer back to this exercise at the very end so please don't worry too much if you don't complete it fully right now however I do want you to take an honest look at yourself and think about "your personal brand" and ask yourself:

- What does my personal brand currently say to others?

- What do I want to do?

- What's working for me and what's not working for me?

- What changes do I need to make to improve my brand?

- What have others said about me in the past that I've just ignored and did they have a point?

- Think long and hard on how you're currently viewed by others and then how you really want other people to see you both in person and online.

- CV and covering letter – make sure you have a solid base to work from that you're happy with and can then adapt for each role you apply for (see free downloads at the end of this book for easy to use templates).

- Online brand – clean up and ramp up your Facebook, twitter, LinkedIn accounts and make sure you add some quality content about yourself and delete any inappropriate photos and add some that are more in line with your new brand image. With LinkedIn ask for some recommendations from ex-colleagues or employers and make sure that your profile matches your CV.

- As well as taking in everything we will cover in the coming chapters undertake your own research and educate yourself further on body language, interview skills, personal branding etc as this can make the world of difference.

- Try and find someone you can role play interviews with – not many people like doing this but believe me it really helps and you don't have to do a whole interview just practicing meeting someone for the first time and getting into a conversation can really give you a boost in confidence.

Don't sweat over this right now as you will learn a great deal more as we go through the other chapters which will help you find the answers to some of these questions. BUT you will be challenged in the very last chapter to take action and I will be mapping out a full TO DO list for you to follow through with.

Rookie Mistake #3:	**"Interviewers don't bother checking you out online before they actually meet you"** – BIG MISTAKE! Any good interviewer, especially agencies will look you up online prior to meeting you and will not be impressed with photos of you or your friends showing off your under wear or downing a bottle of vodka! Sounds silly but it happens and I've even been very surprised by some of the photos some people have put on LinkedIn which is a professional version of Facebook.
Interesting Fact:	93% of the recruiters say that they are likely to look at a candidate's social media behavior.

Chapter 4: What job do you want and what do you have to offer?

Welcome to chapter 4 where I want you to really ask yourself, what job do you really want and what do you have to offer? Even if you're just looking for a job that pays a wage to finance your hobbies or past times you need to target the right positions and companies.

First let's just remind you of what we covered in chapter 3 as you'll need to utilise some of the things you discovered there and in other chapters to help you in this chapter. In chapter 3 we took a close look at your brand – how you present yourself in person and online – remember it is about being realistic and honest about how you will be viewed and the opinions that a potential employer may have even before they meet you.

So let's look at what job you want and what you have to offer.....in this chapter we'll look at 3 key topics:

1. Reasons NOT to spam out your CV

2. Being honest and realistic about the roles you apply for

3. How to gear your application and approach

So why do candidates spam out their CV? Well one of the biggest mistakes that a lot of people make without even realising it is that they believe that scatter gunning their CV out to 100's of companies or applying for every role advertised will better their chances of securing a position. Depending on the type of role that you're looking for then this could certainly work in some cases and there's nothing wrong in that as it can be a numbers game. However, if you're applying for roles that require you to be skilled, qualified or experienced in a certain area and not selected because you're the first one pulled out of the hat then in 9 out of 10 cases you won't be doing yourself any favours working in this manner. As I mentioned before, recruiters and hiring managers are trained and skilled in pre-selection techniques and a CV and cover letter that has been mass produced and spammed out will stick put like a sore thumb. Also CVs that have been sent in for roles or opportunities that are miles apart from what they're actually looking for will also hit the bin or trash folder quicker than you can say delete!

I know the pressure is on to get your CV out there but if you're serious about getting the RIGHT job for you then try and take a step back and really think about your approach and how you'll be received at the other end.

The first thing you need to do is to be totally honest with yourself and ask:

1. Do I really meet the requirements of this role?

2. If not where do I fall short?

3. What would I need to do to get there?

4. Would I require training, qualifications, more experience etc?

5. How could I adapt my CV (without lying) to show that I'm ready to take on this role?

Conducting a SWOT analysis (as outlined in chapter 2) on your skills versus those needed for this role could help you here and give you a better picture of where you need to focus your efforts.

Once you've asked yourself these questions and know where you fall short, there are a number of things you could do before firing off your CV and hoping for the best:

1. Try picking up the phone and speaking to the person recruiting for the role and ask them their thoughts and whether you're CV would be considered even though you don't have the right experience. If not, what advice would they give someone of your background looking to get into this line of work?

2. Research other people in the business already in this type of role and see what their backgrounds are – how did they get to this position? Where did they work before? What qualifications do they have? etc etc. This can easily be done by searching them on www.linkedin.com

3. Speak to and arrange to meet with a recruitment agency who specialise in these types of roles and ask them their opinion and how best to approach getting into this role.

4. If you have the time, use LinkedIn to approach and connect with people in this sector and ask them for their help, you'll be surprised but people like to help other people with career advice if you ask in right manner and not be too pushy.

Research like this will give you more confidence and some answers and ideas on how you could get into this type of position or at least strengthen your case with the hiring managers. If you haven't worked in this sector or position before but would do what it takes to get the chance then you could also try and take some of the risk away from the employer and offer to make some form of sacrifice or a trade off to prove just how much you want it and that you're prepared to take a step sideways or backwards to prove yourself and get a foot in the door such as; take a lower salary or even volunteer for a set period, attend courses on your own time and expense, take a lower position with a view of proving yourself, shadow someone in the role (without pay) for a week or month.

PLEASE DO NOT put false information or bend the truth on your CV in the hope that you'll get the interview and that your personality will

win the day – IT WON'T!!!

Once you have pieced together your evidence of why you're the person for the job you need to embed this into your covering letter and CV. Bullet pointing key areas that you are developing to become more experienced or qualified and include any personal training, coaching, research, work experience etc that will add weight to your application.

Also if you have the confidence rather than just send a CV and hope for the best why not try and secure an interview by calling and introducing yourself to the hiring manager or interviewer and bullet point your experience in the conversation and try closing them by saying "I would be very interested in meeting you to discuss my suitability and your company's requirement in more detail, are you available to meet with me tomorrow at 2pm?" If you don't ask you don't get!

The one thing that I've always believed and will make a great conclusion to this chapter and in fact the whole book, is that the true mark of success is doing what you love to do and having an exceptional life. Although everyone is entitled to this and can have it, when it really comes down to it the truth is we only have ourselves to blame for how we live our lives.

In the next chapter we will be looking at covering letters, CVs and applications in much more detail.

Rookie Mistake #4:	**"Sending out 100's of CVs will increase my chances"** – Maybe but if you throw enough mud at the wall then some will stick, however good recruiters and hiring managers will spot a spammed CV a mile off and file it under B.I.N. Take the time to target the right roles and tailor each cover letter and your CV to that particular position and company.
Interesting Fact:	You don't always have to have years of experience to impress an employer and do great things in your career. What you really need is drive, passion and intuition about what the company has to offer and what you have to offer it.

Chapter 5:   Covering Letters, CV's (Resumes) and Applications

OK we're making great progress and now onto chapter 5 but let's just review chapter 4 where we focussed on the roles you really want and can do and what you have to offer and the real conclusion was that the key to success is doing what you love to do. There's nothing worse than having to drag yourself to a job you hate everyday for 8 to 12 hours a day and in the end only you can change this so make sure you find a job you enjoy which will add value both ways. At the end of this book I have recommended some other great books which are all geared to showing you how to take control and take action to achieve goals and overcome challenges, which I know you'll enjoy.

OK in chapter 5 we will be covering:

1. CV, covering letter and application forms

2. CV structure and content

3. Take action – revamp your CV

OK you're now ready to start applying for positions and arranging interviews and there's a number of ways you can do this.

1. Apply directly to a job advertisement

2. Speculative approach – sending your CV to a company even though they're not advertising

3. Utilise a recruitment agency

4. Be approached by a company or recruiter – head hunted

5. Referral from a friend or family member

As we all know the basic tools utilised to secure an interview are generally a covering letter, CV and the long winded application form.

Application Forms - Some companies still request that you complete an application form in hand written format which is normally to test your reading and writing skills on a basic level but to also make sure your handwriting is legible. Others will because they've always done it that way and like to have it on file and of course to keep HR happy.

Covering letters are a funny one, usually the employer will ask for a covering letter but I have a feeling that not many of them are actually read, maybe skimmed through at best. The best rule of thumb is to include one but keep it brief and to the point. Don't ramble on about how you've always dreamed of working for this company and that this is your dream job etc etc etc. just state the facts, confirm which role you're applying for and maybe bullet point a few key skills and experiences, making sure that they match the job being advertised by using some of the key phrases/terms they used in their advertisement and then let your CV do the talking. If you are sending your CV on a speculative basis then you would need to include a covering letter to explain the reason for you sending in your CV and the type and level of role you're seeking and what you feel you can offer the company. If you're sending this via email then don't double up, use the email as your covering letter rather than writing a separate one and attaching.

CVs - Over the years and especially before the wonders of email I've seen CVs come in all shapes and sizes and they arrive on my desk in many ways. I've had them delivered to me by courier, some came in a boxes, folders, had pull out sections, photos, various addendums, attachments, fold outs, on floppy discs, CDs, USBs, I even had one delivered with a bottle of wine!

My best advice is to keep a CV to a maximum of 3 pages and try and keep it as simple as possible and don't try to be too creative with text boxes, colours, designs etc. Plus there is no real need to include a photo unless requested. With all that said, there's nothing stopping you trying something completely different to get noticed i.e. if you work within the creative space then please use your creativity and imagination to show case your CV. I saw an excellent CV from a very talented web designer which was an actual cartoon story of his CV......I would have given him an interview just to find out how he did it!

Example of CV Structure:

1. Name, Address and Contact Details

Ensure that you use a phone number and email address that you use on a regular basis as you don't want to miss any opportunities or keep an employer waiting by failing to respond to an invitation for an interview. Also remember what we covered regarding using email addresses that might be seen as inappropriate.

2. Overview

Not everyone does this, however it can be a good opportunity to highlight some key experiences/achievements and what you're looking to achieve in your next role and what you feel you can offer to an employer. It's also where you can be a bit more creative and gear this section to each job you apply for as the trained eye will often be attracted to this section to get a feel of the person behind the CV.

3. Skills Summary

Again not everyone does this but it can be another way to highlight some key skills by bullet pointing rather than war and peace and again you can use some of the key words/phrases they utilised in their job advertisement but don't make it too obvious by cutting and pasting their advert!

4. Education, Qualifications and Training

Use your common sense here. If you have an advanced degree, few people are going to be concerned about the exams you took when you were 16 years old. Make sure to also include any training courses that you have done that are relevant to the job that you are applying for. Don't attach endless certificates or proof of qualifications unless requested to do so in the advert as these will be requested when needed.

5. Work Experience

Here you need to cover all your work history both paid and relevant volunteer work or even work experience placements. Always start with your most recent job at the top and work backwards, double check that your dates are correct and don't leave any gaps as this will be picked up on. If you do have some gaps it's best to state a reason so that potential employers don't jump to any conclusions. There's nothing wrong in taking a year out or a career break/change but make sure you include it and show it in a positive light focusing on the fact that it gave you some great alternative skills, experience or knowledge, but don't overdo it.

It's often a good idea to give a very brief overview of each company you worked for just in case they're not known by the reader. Then state what your position was, dates employed, your responsibilities and anything else you feel relevant and again if applicable you could utilise the same phrases and words relevant to the role you're applying for. Some people can actually get stuck putting their duties onto paper without making it sound a bit boring so if you do get stuck take a look at your contract of employment and see if you were given a job description and crib something from there. If your duties were the same at different employers don't put "as above" or "same as previous" as this is lazy, try and show that you've added some experience and grown in the role in some way.

6. Key Achievements

Future employers will be interested to read any key areas where you went above and beyond the call of duty or excelled in areas of the job where you achieved something great. Such as; smashing your sales targets and being No.1 on the leader board for 3 months on the trot, won a trip to New York for best employee of the year, opened an office in a foreign country etc. They don't have to be that far out and remember be proud of your achievements no matter how small they may seem to others.

7. Interests

I'm not that fussed to read in a CV that a candidate likes to go hiking, plays chess, likes to watch movies etc so it's really down to the individual whether to include or not. However if you do an activity out of work that is rather unusual or relevant then definitely include this such as volunteer work for help the homeless, disabled, elderly etc or school governor, travelled overseas to volunteer in a remote village building a church etc. Again please use your common sense here as I have seen people include things that shouldn't be on a CV such as "socialising" i.e. going to the pub, club etc. If you want to show that you like meeting people then the word "networking" is much better received but if you're asked to expand on this at interview don't say "standing at the bar drinking with my mates!"

8. References

I feel it's best to just state that 'References are available on request' Two reasons for this, one you may not want anyone else knowing you're looking for a new job and secondly references are normally taken after the first interview or at offer stage or unless requested prior to the first interview, however I would always suggest that you state that you would prefer to attend an interview before giving anyone permission to start taking references because you might not want the job after meeting them.

Remember there are lots of information that you do not have to include on your CV such as date of birth, age, gender, race, sexual preferences, religion or political views etc and it is illegal for an employer to ask for this information prior to employment.

OK time for more work! Get your CV out or on your screen and have another look at it. Using what you've learnt revamp the main structure and content of the CV and keep as a template (feel free to download the sample templates – see details at the end of this book) ready for when you're ready to apply for a live job. When you see a job you want to apply for copy the template and then adapt it to the role you're applying for adding in key words that are relevant for that role. Do the same with the covering letter.

Rookie Mistake #5:	**"I'll lie on my CV to get the interview and once they meet me they'll want to hire me"** Never lie on your CV, if any credible employer discovers that you were prepared to lie to get the job then what else are you prepared to do? Gearing your CV to match the requirement is fine as long as you're not bending the truth. Some employers or recruiters may word their advert or job description slightly different to what you're used to so utilise the same wording and phrases they've used.

Interesting Fact: The majority of recruiters and hiring managers will take between 6-8 seconds to scan a CV and if it doesn't catch their eye they'll move on very quickly.

Chapter 6: Interview Preparation & Execution

Welcome to chapter 6 and as a result of all your hard work and efforts in following through with what you learnt in chapter 5 such as revamping your covering letters and CVs and how you approach applying for roles, you're now over the first hurdle of securing an interview, good work! However once you've been invited to an interview it's important to remember that this doesn't mean you've got the job, you've got your foot in the door but now you really need to put in the hard work. You've got an opportunity to present your case to show why you are the best candidate for this position and don't forget what we've already discussed; it's also the company's opportunity to show you that they're the right company for you! So in this chapter we're going to cover:

1. Research, research, research

2. Prepare, prepare, prepare

3. Interviews – what you need to know

It really amazes me at just how many candidates still rock up for interviews unprepared or are obviously winging it.....believe me it really does show. You might think that you're one of these people who always get by and somehow seems to land on your feet but this is probably why you're still attending interviews. The candidates who perform the best at interview are the ones who have prepared, researched and come across as passionate about securing the position. The ones who come across the worst and tend to have much shorter interviews are the people who show up with no real understanding, knowledge or interest in the position, the company, their products or services and come across as if they're just going through the motions. Even if the job is not high level or technically challenging, it could even be a pot washer's role – the person who comes across as showing a real interest and some passion will shine through and that could even win over experience. I've hired people with no experience in the role I was hiring for because at interview they showed initiative, passion, desire and hunger to get that job. And the key thing to remember is that the Pot Washer can soon become the Bar Tender and then the Manager and then the Owner!

So what are companies looking to find out from the candidate at the interview?

- Do you have the skills and experience they need and can you do the job?

- Are you motivated to do the job?

- Are you a good fit for their culture and team environment?

- What value can you add to the team, business and their clients?

- Are you a future leader of the business?

Types of interview you may come across:

It's worth trying to find out prior to the interview the type of interview you can expect as they do vary and you need to be able to prepare so it's worth making a point to ask. Some styles of interviews:

- First interview
- Second interview
- Telephone interview or face to face
- One to one or a panel of interviewers
- Questions based on your CV or application form
- Competency based questions
- Case study exercise
- Academic or technical questions
- Assessment centre and selection tests
- Psychometric testing
- Giving a presentation

So before you can start your preparation for the interview you need to find out some important information:

1. **Where is the interview being held and how will you get there with time to spare?** Think about your route, parking, bus stops, tube stations etc. If possible try a test run the day before the interview at the same time of day.

2. **What time is the interview and how long should you allow for this?** If you're parking then you'll need to allow plenty of time just in case you run over as you don't want to appear trying to close the interview because you might get a ticket. If you keep them interested and you want to continue but know your parking is running out, explain politely that you're enjoying the discussion so much you didn't realise the time so could you pop out and put some more money in the meter as you'd love to continue?

3. **Who are you meeting?** This very important as you want to make sure you're meeting the right person plus you can then research their background and position/history with the company. You might be meeting 2 or 3 people in which case you might need to prepare more than one copy of any samples of work, presentations, CVs etc. Plus you won't be so surprised if you walk into a room and suddenly discover you're heavily outnumbered.

4. **Which role are you interviewing for?** Seems a silly question but it's best to make sure that you and the interviewer are on the same page.

5. **How will you start the conversation if need be?**

6. **What questions will they ask you and how will you respond?** It's a good idea to think of any curve ball questions they may have about gaps in your CV, why you left your last job, why you want this job, why should they chose you etc.

7. **What do you know about their company?** Nearly every interviewer will ask this question and it is very important that you have something to say to show how much interest you have in joining the company. We will cover this in much more detail shortly.

8. **What questions will you ask them?**

Don't be afraid to pick up the phone and ask someone some questions but it would be prudent not to ask the person you're due to meet. You could always speak to the receptionist or ask to speak to their marketing department and be honest and tell them that you have a meeting and would like some information to help prepare for your meeting and I'm sure they would be prepared to help you out.

Make sure you know your CV inside out and have copies with you Make sure you've revised your dates of employment, reasons for leaving and ensure that you can expand on your original application. Revise the job specification and familiarise yourself with what the employer will be looking for from the ideal candidate.

Before you even step into the interview room the first two things you must do are..........

1. **RESEARCH, RESEARCH, RESEARCH!!**

2. **PREPARE, PREPARE, PREPARE!!**

I really want to ram these points home to you because I want you to understand just how important they really are. The thing is, it's not that hard and in fact if you're interested in securing a good job with a good company then let's face it - it's a MUST! You don't want to work for some crappy company who might not even pay you or don't offer any advancement or long term development or you regret joining 2 weeks later, so take the time, the effort and the interest and do some research. Here are some basic questions to research prior to interview and the information you find out can be used when asked what do you know about the company at interview plus you can also use or expand on them when they ask if you have any questions:

• When was the company established and by whom?

- What are the key miles stones or successes in their journey/history to date?

- What do they specialise in? (services/products etc)

- What is the company structure? (Find or ask for a company organogram)

- What are the company's growth strategies/plans or new products/ services etc?

- What is the background of the person/people you're meeting?

- Who else works there that you might know?

- What are the backgrounds of people in similar roles that you're applying for?

- Who are their top 3 competitors and how do they differ?

Once you start asking you can go on forever and a day and there are normally a few questions that lead on from each of these, which we call probing questions to get more detail behind the answer.

With all the technology and information available at a push of a button it's very easy to find out some basic information about the people you're meeting to not only give you some confidence but also ideas on topics to discuss or areas to use during the interview. LinkedIn is a very powerful tool for this and it's free! Plus you can often find a profile of the person on the company's website or simply Google them to see what comes up and of course you can often see some basic information on Facebook even if you're not friends.

Be sensible and professional with this and make sure that anything you use is not sensitive or inappropriate. Also when you enter the reception or the persons office always be aware of photos, awards, football team memorabilia or even a set of golf clubs tucked in the corner, anything that can help open up the conversation and make you both feel at ease and get off on the right foot.

What questions will they ask you?

It's important that you think long and hard about this and be ready for anything. There are two main types of questions which would be used at interview which are general and competency. General questions tend to be open such as "tell me about yourself?", "what are your strengths and weaknesses?" It is a good idea to think about what you would say and say it out loud. This will help you to refine your thoughts and practise being clear and concise. Competency based questions test your skills and experience such as "describe a time when..." Typical competencies include creativity, analytical skills, teamwork, and leadership so make sure you research the competencies that the role requires and you can find these either in the job specification or advertisement. Employers like to see/hear evidence to back up an answer so make sure you can give a couple of good examples to illustrate your point.

Some common interview questions include:

- Tell me about yourself?
- Why do you want this job?
- Why did you leave your last job?
- What is your greatest strength and greatest weakness?
- Describe a difficult work situation and how you overcame it.
- What motivates and de-motivates you?
- Describe the best boss for you
- Why did you leave your last employer?
- Why would we choose you over our other candidates?
- What will you bring to the business now and in the future?

What will you ask them and what do you really need to know?

- What else can you tell me about the business?
- What is the business strategy for the next 5 years?
- How many staff do you currently have and growth plans?
- What is the staff turnover?
- What training can you offer someone like me?
- What long term career opportunities are available?
- What is the reason for the vacancy? If someone left ask why?
- How would you describe a typical day in this role?
- How will I be measured in my role?
- How often do you conduct reviews and performance appraisals?
- Who would I report into? What is their background?
- What are your expectations of me?
- What challenges do you think I will face?
- If this is a sales role ask about targets/KPIs, commission/bonus structure, how the team is doing against targets and why hitting or not.

The list is endless and depends on how much time you have but make sure you get the answers to the questions you really need to know.

So what shouldn't you ask at 1st interview? You will be surprised at how many people will only ask certain questions that show they're in it for the money or an easy life such as:

- What does your company do?
- How many days holiday can I take? – OK you will need to know but don't make it a priority at first interview.
- How many sick days can I take?
- When will I get a pay rise?
- How soon will I be promoted?
- How much do you earn?
- Can I leave early on Fridays as I always meet with friends for drinks?
- Can I have Wednesday afternoons off as I play football and we train before the match?
- How many hours will I be expected to work?

First impressions count...

The average length of an interview will be around 40 minutes, but 33% of 2000 surveyed recruiters by LinkedIn said that they know within the very first 90 seconds of the interview if they will recruit the candidate. Its good practice to think of your-self on show the minute you leave the house and head to the interview. You could easily encounter an employee of the company or even the person interviewing you on the way there or when you're parking in their car park or waiting in reception, so always be polite and think before you speak as there's no worse way to start a meeting or interview to suddenly discover your interviewer is the other driver you made a rude gesture to or swore at in the car park....sounds silly but believe me this happens.

Dress Code...

In most cases the first impression you make will be the most important and is generally based on how you look and what you are wearing. Therefore regardless of the work environment its best practice to dress professionally for an interview. Even if you've heard that they wear casual clothes most days you still want to stand out from the crowd and make a good impression. Some tips on what to wear would include:

For Men:

- Suit – solid colours such as black, navy, grey etc.

- Smart polished shoes
- Belt – not with a Harley Davidson logo or skull & cross bones
- Long sleeve shirt with co-ordinated tie
- Conservative socks - not The Simpsons
- Tidy hair style
- Remove any piercings
- Cut your finger nails and don't wear too much jewellery (preferably none)
- Briefcase – try not to take a rucksack

For Women:

- Suit – solid colours such as black, navy, grey etc.
- Skirt should be a comfortable length when sitting
- Blouse
- Shoes – conservative and try to avoid shoes with too high heels
- Limit the jewellery and make up where possible
- Tidy hair style
- Manicured nails
- Briefcase or portfolio

And always remember to take with you:
- The directions for where you're going
- A pen and note pad
- A copy of your CV
- A copy of the advert or job description
- Your research on the company and questions for the interviewer
- Any examples of work that you would like to present
- Take your mobile in case you need to call ahead or they need to contact you however...
- TURN YOUR PHONE OFF – better still leave it in the car or put it away

During the interview:

- Sit upright and do not fidget in the seat
- Keep your hands on show

- Maintain good eye contact
- Keep an open posture
- Minimise things you do when nervous i.e. play with pen, tap fingers on desk etc
- Make sure you understand the question before responding
- Speak clearly and don't rush your answer
- Always make notes but ask them if they don't mind before hand
- Remember to breathe!

Poor body language that can put the interviewer off of a candidate:

- Playing with something on the desk/table
- Having bad posture i.e. slumping in the chair or legs open
- Fidgeting too much in their seats
- Crossing their arms over their chests
- Playing with their hair or touching their face
- Having a weak or too strong handshake
- Using too many hand gestures

Closing the Interview:

Unless prompted by the interviewer, the majority of candidates being interviewed will leave the interview not knowing how they got on, what the next stage will be or how long it will take for a decision. Which is why you should always ask and in fact it won't do you any harm and will show you're interested and keen to move onto the next phase. Example of questions to ask:

- What is the next stage?
- When will I hear if I've been successful?
- How many other candidates are you meeting?
- When are you looking for someone to start in the position?
- Are there any reservations you have that I can cover whilst I'm here?

And if you want to be a bit cheeky......"When can I start?"

Whatever happens make sure that you always remember to thank them for their time and that you're very keen to progress to next stage or secure the position (if that is the case) and that you look forward to contributing to the team and the business.

Finally, just because the interview is over remember you're still on show so leave in the same manner. Say thank you to the receptionist and leave the building and car park in an orderly fashion. Don't jump up and down congratulating yourself or fist pumping the air just yet wait until you're home!

Good work – now you're ready for the next chapter!

Rookie Mistake #6:	**"I've never had to prepare for an interview because I'm good at thinking on my feet and my personality shines through"** - Rocking up to an interviewing and playing it by ear is a major mistake but you'd be surprised by how many people still do this. Turning up late because you got lost, not knowing who you're meeting and why, not having any questions or knowing anything about the company is probably why you're still attending so many interviews and not getting any offers!
Interesting Fact:	Remember you will be interviewed by another human being! Sounds obvious but most people fear the interviewer and place them in a massive position of power. You have to remember that they have feelings too and much like yourself they've had to prepare for this meeting and could also be nervous and have pressures you don't know about. So relax and enjoy meeting someone new and treat it as a two way discussion or voyage of discovery.

Chapter 7:   Follow up, Feed Back, Negotiation & Resigning

OK we're now on the last real learning chapter before I hand everything over to you to create your own strategy and put everything you've learnt into practice. We've covered a huge amount and there was a lot for you to take in so please take your time and go back at your leisure but use the information wisely and you'll get great results!

In chapter 7 we are going to cover the final stages of the job interview process:

1. Follow up & feed back

2. Negotiation

3. Resigning

Follow up and feed back:

As outlined in previous chapters, don't be afraid to ask any questions especially when they relate to your performance at the interview and the same rule applies after the interview. You are well within your rights to know how you performed – good or bad and you need to learn from it ready for the next interview.

Firstly make sure that you always follow up within 24 hours of the interview either with an email or a call to thank them once again for their time and express your interest in the position and if not discussed at the end of the interview you can also ask if or when a decision will be made.

Remember all feedback is good feedback and if you're informed that you were not suitable DON'T take offense and get into a debate or argument or take it personally, but you do need to know the reasons why. Tell them that you're disappointed that you weren't successful as you were very keen on working for the company but you understand and respect their decision, however as a way of assisting you to move forward you would really welcome their comments and key reasons for not selecting you so that you can learn from this. Most employers will give you a response and this is when you really need to listen and learn so that you can be ready for the next interview. Plus if you don't ask then you'll never know what the response will be and the reason could be something that they misunderstood or could be something that could be rectified.

If when you speak to them a decision is still yet to be made, make sure that you don't hound them, stalk them on social media or make a nuisance of yourself but still ask them about how you performed at interview and if there were any other questions that they might have since the interview that you could answer now.

Other good questions to ask either at the end of the interview or when gaining feedback would be:

- What reservations if any do you have about me in this role?
- On a scale of 1 to 5 (5 being the best) how do I compare to the other candidates you interviewed?
- When should I expect a decision on the next stage?

And my favourite "When can I start?"

Negotiating:

Once you have made it through the selection process and have been informed that you are their No.1 choice for the role and they want to offer you the position, now is the time to keep your head and don't get too excited and give away the farm! If they start asking you how much salary/ package you need to accept for this role, hit the ball back into their court and ask what they had in mind or what would they be prepared to offer a candidate of your calibre. If you've already discussed a figure at interview that was acceptable to you then revert back to that discussion or if they had advertised the role with a salary banding then say the top end of the banding and work from there.

Some good advice is to always try and take time out once an offer has been made, even for an hour or two. Take the time to run everything back through your mind and confirm that everything is the right for you. Good employers won't have an issue with this – just be very polite and thank them for their offer which you're very excited about but you'd like to take a little time to consider everything. This will also be important if you do have other opportunities to consider and the time should be used to inform any other potential employers or agencies that you've received another offer which can help with the decision process.

If you've secured the offer via an agency then the majority of offers will be made through them which will make it a bit easier for you as you can discuss the value of the offer or potential room for negotiation with the recruiter who would then negotiate on your behalf.

But be warned, some recruiters (only a very few!) will just want the placement and want you to accept so they can chalk the placement on the board, however also remember chapter 1, recruiters fees are based on a percentage of what salary you get from the employer so the higher your salary the higher their fee. Recruiters are well trained in negotiating and will know their clients expectations and therefore they would have gauged how keen the client is on securing you when the offer was made. Some will ask "OK Mr Client I'll offer him $80,000 however I know that he was looking for closer to $90,000 so what should we do if they decline, is there room for negotiation?"

Resigning:

OK so you've accepted your offer and are ready to celebrate however before that you now have to resign! This can be very hard for some people because they don't like to let others down and of course others can't wait to kick down the boss's door and tell them what they think of them!

Firstly, keep your head and don't do anything that will bite you back later down the track. Also you must remember why you wanted to leave in the first place. So before you resign you need to prepare and try and pre-empt the conversation and what your boss will say or how they will respond. What reason will you give for leaving and why didn't you mention this before. Don't make it personal or emotional and remember that it's a small world so you don't want to burn your bridges so try and keep a positive spin on things even if you have to bite your tongue, remember you may need a reference from them, you might meet them again or they could know someone in the company you're joining. The fact that you've made a decision to leave and are actually doing it and joining a new business should be reward enough so enjoy the moment without burning the bridges.

Before you resign check your employment contract for your notice period and any holidays you have left then write your resignation letter and make it short and sweet (see free downloads at the end of this book for templates) and state the resignation date and departure date. A few other tips:

- Tell your boss face to face rather than over email or phone

- Although you don't have to give exact reasons for resigning try and be constructive rather than negative as they should learn from this as well, such as lack of training, limited promotion etc.

- You shouldn't make it awkward or uncomfortable for the colleagues you leave behind remember that they still have to work there and might be your friends

- Never resign when you're angry or having a bad day

- Legally you must work your notice period however if you don't want to be there then negotiate to take any holiday owing during the notice period

This is also when you might find out that they really don't want you to leave and could make you a counter offer. Whilst this is very flattering and is a very common reason why a number of people end up staying put, however in my experience a high percentage regret it down the line as the promises made are either not met or the same issues are there. Common counter offers include:

- We'll match their offer

- We were going to promote you to management

- We'll fix those issues etc

The other key thing to remember or to ask yourself is why did it take your resignation for them to make you these promises/increases now? Employers should be holding regular reviews with their staff to understand their needs and to ensure that they are happy (or not) and addressing any issues before they become an even bigger issue and the person leaves.

Generally once you've decided to leave (for the right reasons) it's time to leave and believe me in most cases employers may entice and succeed in changing your mind however you can be assured that they're not going to be happy knowing that you've been speaking to other companies behind their backs or were prepared to go and work for the competition. So commit to what you set out to do and head off into the horizon.

Now don't get me wrong there may well be cases where a counter offer does actually deliver the result that you wanted with your current employer and you stay there but please never use offers from other companies as a way of gaining power with your current employer as its very unprofessional, risky and unfair on the company who thought you were going to join them and we all know it's a small world!

So now you have your new offer and contract signed, resigned from your current position and serving your notice, you can celebrate!

Rookie Mistake #7:	**"If the company doesn't call me back that means I didn't get the job so I should move on"** – This might be the case but you should always follow up as it shows you are proactive and sometimes there might be a genuine reason why they hadn't made contact yet. Also asking for feedback especially when you didn't get the job is a positive thing and any good interviewer will respect this and give you their feed-back so you can learn for the next time.
Interesting Fact:	**49% of job applicants never negotiate offers and just say "Thanks I'll take it" where as those who did negotiate managed to increase their annual income by an average of $5,000.**

Chapter 8:   Call to Action – YOUR NEW STRATEGY!

OK you're on the final chapter congratulations! You now have a much better understanding of how recruitment companies work which will give you more confidence when dealing with them and how to get them working for you. You also have the right frame of mind and confidence to sell your story and your brand, you also have a winning CV and covering letter which you can adapt for each role you apply for and you also have the skills and knowledge on how to present yourself and conduct killer interviews as well as being able to ask all the right questions and even have the skills to close the interview in a way that will leave you knowing one way or the other how things actually went.

Throughout all 7 chapters I've done all the hard work and now it's your turn. I said at the start of this book that to get the best out of this YOU must take action. If you want to achieve anything you need to take a step forward and make it happen, so here we go. I have created a "To Do" list to help get you started and put everything you've learnt into practice. You can delete or add to it whatever you like but just make sure that you have an action plan that you commit to and will follow through with as this will get you results much sooner than you think and like I say if you do nothing then nothing will happen. Let's get started:

1. Re-vamp and simplify your CV and covering letter as outlined in chapter 5. Check out some current or older adverts/job descriptions for key words and phrases.

2. If you have a Facebook page go in and have an honest look and freshen it up a bit and make it look more appropriate, deleting any photos that you think might be viewed as inappropriate.

3. If you don't already have a LinkedIn account then create one it's free for a basic account, just go to *www.linkedin.com* Your LI page is very similar to a CV but accessib le by millions of potential employers and useful contacts plus 1000's of jobs are advertised and employers search LI for candidates who match their requirements. Recent figures (Nov 2015) showed LI having over 400 million members!! And their target is 1 Billion. Take time to create a well written profile page (not war and peace) and use a professional photo – not one of you and the kids or at the pub. Whilst you're creating your page you can search other people in similar roles to see how they present themselves but try and be original as not all profiles are great.

4. Once you have a LinkedIn account start to research/search people in roles and companies you'd be keen to work for and target yourself to connect with a number of key people in your industry. Don't just send the standard "I'd like to connect with you" be more creative and sincere – I've created a template for you on how to approach and create LinkedIn connections. Also follow companies that are relevant as this

adds value as you'll see what they're up to and any vacancies they advertise.

5. Again you can do this on LinkedIn or any way you wish but research and select two recruitment firms that specialise in your sector preferably within travelling distance so that you can meet them face to face. Make contact and arrange to meet with the relevant consultant at both. Remember they're always looking for good candidates so if pushed for a CV before meeting give them a brief overview over the phone and say that you're writing your CV and will send it once it's finished but as you're extremely busy and time is of the essence let's put a time in the diary to meet. Check your LI account the day after and see if they've viewed your profile! Make sure you view theirs.

6. When you meet with the recruiters get the answers to the questions we ran through in chapter 1 and ask them for as much advice and assistance as you can on your CV presentation, interview techniques and their thoughts in general. A good recruiter will be honest but constructive and remember any feedback is good feedback so learn from it. Make sure you mention to the recruiter if you are working with another recruiter and which firms they are approaching on your behalf and which ones you are approaching yourself. They may ask you to sign a confirmation which outlines the companies they will approach on your behalf as this will protect their fee. Make sure you come away with an agreed plan of action with that recruiter on exactly who they are going to approach or vacancies they will put you forward for and the timescales in which they will keep you updated on progress and then hold them to this – if they don't call you or email you by the agreed timescale make contact with them.

7. Make sure that you have a number of companies you can approach yourself as it's good to be involved and also some companies won't like paying recruiter's fees and would be pleased to hear from you directly. Research them before approaching to see if you can find an edge and a way of standing out from other applicants.

8. Rehearse your interview technique either by running through by yourself out aloud or with a friend – if you build a good relationship with your recruiter and they arrange an interview with one of their clients ask them if you could come in and run through your interview preparation with them. Try different ways of getting the initial introduction, handshake and conversation starter and then focus running through what questions they might ask you and rehearse your answers and then how you will end and leave the meeting.

9. Research, research & research and then prepare, prepare & prepare before every interview – it will make the world of difference and will give you the confidence you need to compete with other candidates and NAIL THAT JOB!

10. Last and most importantly, enjoy the process and learn from every knock back or rejection you receive so that you can change your approach the next time round, don't let it drag you down and make you negative which will show in your manner when speaking to others about your experiences. Remember what Albert Einstein said **"Insanity: doing the same thing over and over again and expecting different results."**

Well that is it from me! I hope you enjoyed this book and are now raring to get stuck into your new job search adventure.

If like me you get a kick out of helping other people then please visit our website page at **www.jobinterviewgamechanger.com** or **www.facebook. com/jobinterviewgamechanger** or Linkedin pages and press "like" or please recommend this book or **The Job Interview Game Changer** to your friends, family or colleagues.

Also as I will be improving and updating the book as I learn along the process and would be keen to add reader's experiences and stories in the updated versions so if you'd like a mention then please write to me and let know how things work out for you. **support@jobinterviewgamechanger. com**

Take care and enjoy your new career!

Chris Bell

Acknowledgments

During my career I've been extremely lucky to have worked with and made friends with so many great people who have taught me, mentored me, motivated me, inspired me, bollocked me, made me laugh and driven me to become the person I am today and whilst I can't name everyone, I did want to make a special thank you to just a few people or we could be here all day - so a big thank you to Stephen Hill, Steven Ware, Gary Nash, Owen Goodhead, Danny Dobson and of course everyone else that I've worked with and known over the years as you've all added value to my learning experience and I've enjoyed every step of the journey.

Further Inspiration:

I've added some recommended reading for you after this section but I also wanted to give you a few of the great one liners that have always caught my eye over the years and have stuck with me and often help kick start my day or perk me up when things are going against the grain:

"A real decision is measured by the fact that you've taken a new action. If there's no action, you haven't truly decided." – Tony Robbins

"By believing in his dreams, man turns them into reality" – Hergé

"Whether you think you can or you think you can't, you're right." – Henry Ford

"Remember no one can make you feel inferior without your consent." – Eleanor Roosevelt

"I can't change the direction of the wind, but I can adjust my sails to always reach my destination." – Jimmy Dean

"Nothing is impossible; the word itself says 'I'm possible'!" – Audrey Hepburn

"Too many of us are not living our dreams because we are living our fears." – Les Brown

"When everything seems to be going against you, remember that the airplane takes off against the wind, not with it." – Henry Ford

"Identify your problems, but give your power and energy to solutions." – Tony Robbins

"Do or do not. There is no try." – Yoda

Some Recommended Reading:

Although these titles are not specifically geared to job seeking as such, they have however inspired me over my career and more recently to put pen to paper and write this book. If you are looking to change your life and live what is known as an "exceptional life" – living and working on your terms! then I'm sure that you will get just as much out of these as I did....

- Unlimited Power – Anthony Robbins
- Awaken the Giant Within – Anthony Robbins
- Rich Dad Poor Dad – Robert T Kiyosaki
- 6 months to 6 figures – Peter Voogd
- The 4 Hour Work Week – Tim Ferriss
- Crush It! - Gary Vaynerchuk

BONUS WORD FORMATTED TEMPLATES:

- Call to action - Your TO DO sheet
- Covering letter template
- CV template
- Interview Planner
- How to negotiate the offer
- Letter of resignation
- How to connect with LI members

To claim your FREE word formatted templates simply enter your name and "free templates" in the subject box of an email and send to support@jobinterviewgamechanger.com

www.ingramcontent.com/pod-product-compliance
Lightning Source LLC
Chambersburg PA
CBHW070335190526
45169CB00005B/1901